Jarrold Collectors Series

Let's Collect
British Gemstones
with text by **Sam Weller**

Jarrold Colour Publications, Norwich

Introduction

Gemstones are fascinating natural objects. Little knowledge is needed to find and prize attractive specimens, but to fully appreciate their many-faceted interest some delving into at least three specialisations is helpful — mineralogy, geology and jewellery.

Harsh selection was inevitable in the compilation of this small book, *Let's Collect British Gemstones*. Scottish examples are already covered by *Let's Look at Scottish Gemstones*.

Gemstones and Minerals

The British Isles, a tiny fraction of the land surface, produces a large number of mineral species because most rock types are represented in Britain. All of the illustrations given are British mineral species or gem-rocks. A few well-known names, i.e. diamond and sapphire, are absent because they do not occur, or are very rare, in Britain. The fringe species of organic origin, jet, amber, coral and pearls, are excluded.

What is a mineral? — simply 'a naturally occurring inorganic chemical compound or element'. Thus, common table salt (sodium chloride) from a manufacturing chemist is not a mineral, but halite from a Cheshire salt-mine is; refined copper is not, but a piece of native copper in the rocks is. There are about 2,500 mineral species and a much larger number of varietal forms (small but defined variations in chemical composition as, for example, in the various types and colours of tourmaline). Notably certain metals, e.g. iron and magnesium, are prone to substitute for one another in their compounds thus modifying the end product into a totally different species.

The word 'rock' has specialist meaning. Rocks are assemblages of mineral grains. Untypically, rocks may be composed of a single mineral type; for example, quartz rock. Granite (grain-ite), an igneous example, is more usual. Here the cooling rock fluid (magma) has frozen into grains of quartz and feldspar, and often additional minerals, to form the solid hard rock.

Stone is an old word loosely used to describe all the hard inorganic constituents of our world. The better terms Precious Minerals, Gem-Rocks, and Ornamental Stone, will be used in this book.

Precious Minerals and Gem-Rocks

Less than a hundred mineral types are commonly used in jewellery and artistic work. There are three properties required of a precious mineral — beauty, hardness and scarcity. Beauty is hard to define, but obvious. Hardness is a practical requirement to resist wear and damage. Scarcity affects our judgment of value. In the booming new application for mineral pieces — decor specimens — perfection, not rarity, is the main criteria.

Some precious minerals — native gold, native silver, lapis-lazuli and turquoise, for example, have attracted our attention since earliest times. In contrast, as recently as 1967 a newly-discovered violet/blue variety of zoisite from Tanzania has entered the jeweller's inventory, appropriately as tanzanite. Traditionally, jewellers, have divided gem-minerals between precious and semi-precious stones. (The term 'stone' is always applied to cut specimens for incorporation into jewellery.)

Most of the British material is 'semi-precious' and in the quartz family. Somewhat arbitrarily some material, both minerals and rocks (usually of lower quality) is described as Gem-Rock.

How Minerals Form

This is a specialist topic but the key notions are more unfamiliar than difficult to understand.

'Rocks are minerals', or are formed of mineral grains, and so we must first consider how rocks are formed. There are three major rock families — Magmatic (or Igneous), Sedimentary and Metamorphic. Magma is the hot viscous material formed in the lower levels of the earth's crust. When magma cools slowly (under the surface) coarse-grained, crystalline rocks result. A magma rich in silica (acidic) produces granitic rocks. Conversely, low silica content but high iron/magnesium content (basic) yields gabbraic types. Magma reaching the surface is lava which usually cools quickly to produce the fine-grained types of rhyolite and basalt respectively. The minerals in a granite or rhyolite are quartz and feldspar. Gabbros and basalts comprise feldspar and various iron/magnesium silicates (ferro-magnesian silicates) usually olivine, hornblende or pyroxene.

Sedimentary rocks are in a sense 'second-hand', being comprised of the re-cemented grains (usually under water) of the eroded debris from earlier rocks. Familiar examples are Sandstone, Shale, Chalk and Limestone, though the latter two are less obviously due to erosion since they comprise fossil debris.

Metamorphosis is the unnerving title to the processes by which gradual changes take place in both magmatic and sedimentary rocks. Often change is so gradual that the outward form is hardly altered and it is only the chemical composition that changes — that is to say, a new suite of constituent minerals is born. Soft mudstones formed in the cool, low-pressure environment of an ancient seabed are metamorphosed into hard, perfect cleaving slates due to the pressures involved in earth movements. The glassy feldspars in a granite may slowly be transmuted into soft microscopic crystals of kaolin (china clay) by acidic rain waters, or, alternatively, the gem-mineral tourmaline by hot boron-rich vapours.

Mineral Forming Environments

Many minerals, notably the 'rock-forming silicates', derive directly from cooling magma. The sedimentary rocks, because of their secondary origin, yield fewer pure species. Numerous species, however, are produced in originally sedimentary rocks by metamorphism — including garnets and rubies.

It is the vein minerals that provide most of the metalliferous and many of the gem species. These vein minerals are crystallised into fissures of the rocks (of all types) from the hot mineralised fluids that are left in the final phase of the formation of magmatic rocks. Different minerals form in the progressively lower bands of temperature during cooling. Avoiding inappropriate complexity, the temperature range may be divided and labelled as:

Pegmatic, Hot Solutions, Circulating Waters and Evaporates.

Pegmatic

The last portion of a cooling magma will have a higher content of the elements not used to form the usual rock-forming silicate minerals. These 'late fluids' have special crystal growth-promoting properties, hence the pegmatite veins they form are often the source of large wellformed crystals of rare minerals. Pegmatites are the source of many of the world's gems.

Hot Solutions

Below pegmatic temperatures most of the silicate material has been used and it is the metalliferous minerals of economic importance that start to form. At the top of the range tin, wolfram and molybdenum are 'compounded', while at the low temperature end the lead and antimonal minerals are formed.

Circulating Waters and Evaporates

Even cold water can give rise to extensive mineralisation. Hundreds of feet depth of carbonate minerals have resulted from the age-long action of surface waters dissolving limestone beds and then precipitating out at a distance. Many exotic minerals owe their formation to the chemical activities of surface waters working down through the upper parts of mineral lodes (the oxidisation zone) and modifying the original minerals.

The slow evaporation of ancient lakes and inland seas has resulted in the formation of salt-domes.

Where to Look

All of us have the collector's instinct in varying degree, and there is the added bonus with mineral collecting that it provides interest with out-of-doors activity. One must accept that most of the superb examples in museums and mineral dealers' stocks have derived from working mines and quarries (often a century or so ago before the introduction of high explosives). Don't be deterred, you will find in the more fruitful areas specimens you will treasure. On the inside cover is a location map giving some of the especially good British collecting areas. Individual sites are not listed. Some useful addresses appear at the back of this book. Once in an area seek local knowledge, but above all consider the formative processes by which minerals grow and apply your own judgement. In the likely areas, anywhere rocks are exposed — river beds, cliffs, beaches, mine tips and quarries, plus road workings — are potential hunting grounds. Apply common sense and courtesy. Some localities are potentially dangerous, especially to children and animals. Above all, do not trespass or vandalise.

The prime difficulty is not collecting, but identification of finds. Detailed information on species diagnosis is beyond this small book's aims. However, with the illustrations and the accompanying descriptions you will certainly be able to make a good start towards naming most of the British gem species you find.

Chemical and Physical Properties

Minerals, and hence gems, are classified into families based on their common chemical properties. The universally adopted system, with minor modification, was proposed by the American mineralogist Edward Dana. There are, in the usual form, ten groups. Not every group contains gem species:

Native elements	— Gold, Silver, Diamond
Sulphides and Sulphasalts	— Pyrite, Marcasite, Sphalerite
Oxides and Hydroxides	— Quartz, Ruby, Haematite
Halides	— Fluorspar
Carbonates	— Malachite, Azurite, Rhodochrosite
Nitrates and Borates	— Colmanite
Sulphates	— Baryte
Phosphates, Vanadates, Arsenates	— Brazillianite, Turquoise, Apatite
Tungstates, Molybdates, Uraniates	— Scheelite
Silicates	— Chrysocolla, Dioptase

The chemical properties of minerals at this first level of discussion cannot be seen to assume importance. However, the physical properties are directly evident and must be discussed.

Hardness — a measure of scratch resistance.

There are different forms of hardness and some minerals have different values along different directions. The hardness scale (defined by

Mohs) has ten (unequal) steps standardised by common minerals. A mineral on the scale will scratch anything equal or below.

1. Talc
2. Gypsum
3. Calcite (rhom face)
4. Fluorite
5. Apatite
6. Feldspar
7. Quartz
8. Topaz
9. Corundum
10. Diamond

Streak — is the colour of the finely powdered mineral.
Minerals up to about 7 (Mohs scale) are tested by scratching an unglazed light-coloured tile.

Fracture — the broken surface of a mineral is characteristic.
The fracture type names are self explanatory except 'conchoidal' which is a curved shell-shaped, glassy break.

Cleavage — most minerals tend to break along flat, smooth planes in response to carefully applied investigative pressure. The property is fundamental and depends on the sub-microscopic atomic arrangements that generate the minerals' crystallographic properties.

Specific Gravity — is the weight of a mineral compared with the same volume of water. It is a simply measured but important diagnostic property.

The most important optical properties are:

Colour — is a familiar and important mineral property but can be a misleading guide to identification. Although some minerals, malachite for example, have constant colour, others, such as quartz, may be almost any colour. Physically, colour depends on the transmission and absorption of light of different wavelengths passing through the substance.

Adulorescence — is the bluish sheen exhibited by certain minerals, notably Labradorite; it is due to the microscopic alignment of internal crystals.

Pleochroism — some coloured and transparent species, notably tourmaline and andalucite, beryl and ruby, appear to change colour when viewed in different directions.

Refraction — light entering a transparent material from air is bent. The whole practice of gem-cutting seeks to exploit the effect by maximising the amount of light aimed back to the observer's eye. The popular term is 'fire'.

CRYSTALS

Crystallography, the study of crystals, is a specialised topic of large, practical importance, but unless sufficient information can be presented, the topic seems just a jumble of obscure definitions. This small book does not attempt to explain crystal classification beyond tabulating the six axial systems and indicating the axial conventions.

When minerals grow from a melt (solidify from the molten state) or separate out from a solution (crystallise) they develop, under the ideal conditions of adequate supply, sufficient time and space, the remarkable smooth-faced angular shapes we know as crystals.

The faces of crystals (smooth surfaces) have exact and unalterable angular relationships, regardless of crystal size. These relationships are the visible result of the sub-microscopic atomic and molecular structures called the crystal-lattice. It is, in fact, the possession of a crystal-lattice that defines the so-called solid state of matter and all of the physical properties already mentioned result from these lattice arrangements.

The ideal conditions required for the growth of large, well-formed crystals are rare yet a quartz crystal of 40 tons weight is reported from the U.S.S.R.

Crystallographers assign all known mineral crystals into just six systems. We shall be content to observe that each of the six systems is related to an axial system (in solid geometry) that facilitates the spatial determination and reporting of crystal faces.

1. Cubic   **5.** Orthorhombic

2. Hexagonal   **6.** Triclinic

3. Monoclinic

4. Tetragonal

In the field, minerals assume an initially bewildering range of appearances. A given mineral species invariably crystallises in its 'system' (one of the six), but there are a range of 'forms' which it may adopt. The common mineral iron pyrite is frequently encountered as cubes or pyritohedra, and, less frequently, in other forms. Iron pyrite is in the cubic system and the term 'habit' is used to indicate which of the forms predominate in a given example.

Other phenomena, distorted growth, parallel growth and twinning, may all assist in producing a diverse range of appearances.

Cubic Three equal axis (a, a₂, a₃) all at right angles to each other

Hexagonal Four axis, the principal (c-axis) is at right angles to the other three which are in a common plane and 120° apart

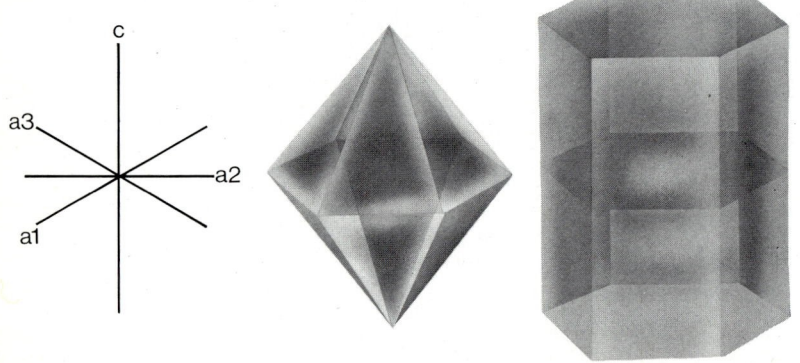

Monoclinic Three unequal axis at 90° to the plane of a and c

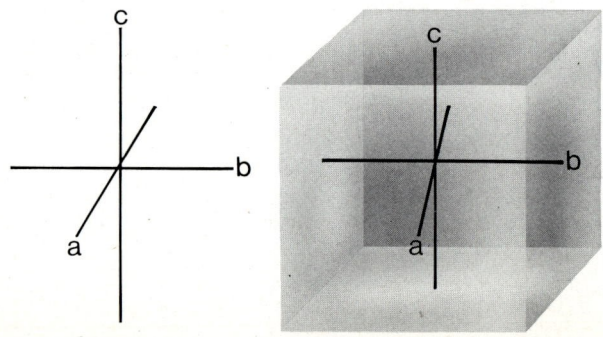

Tetragonal Two unequal axis (a, a₂) at 90° to each other and the main c-axis

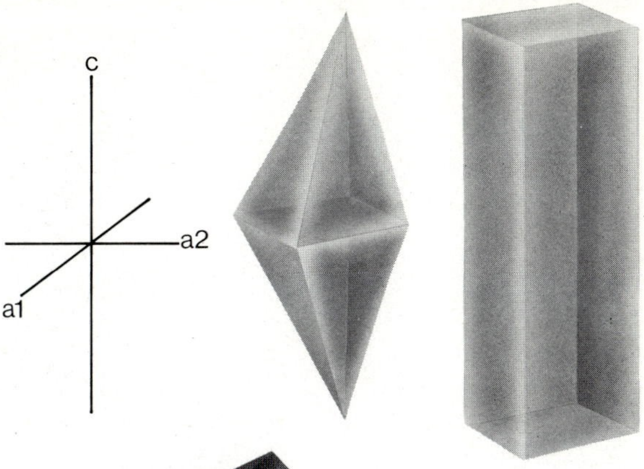

Orthorhombic The axis, each unequal, all at 90° to each other

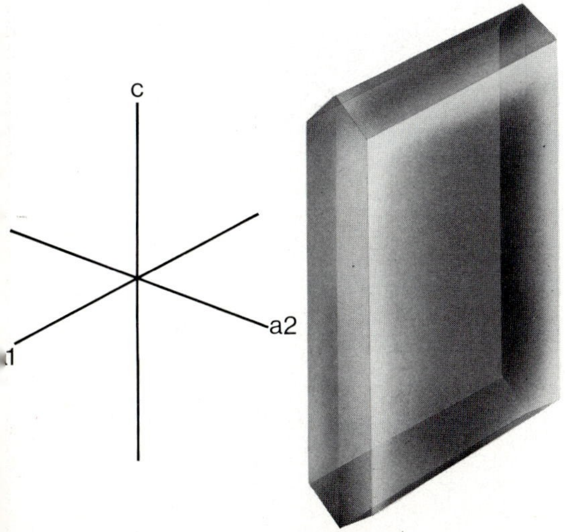

Triclinic Three unequal axis all at obtuse angles

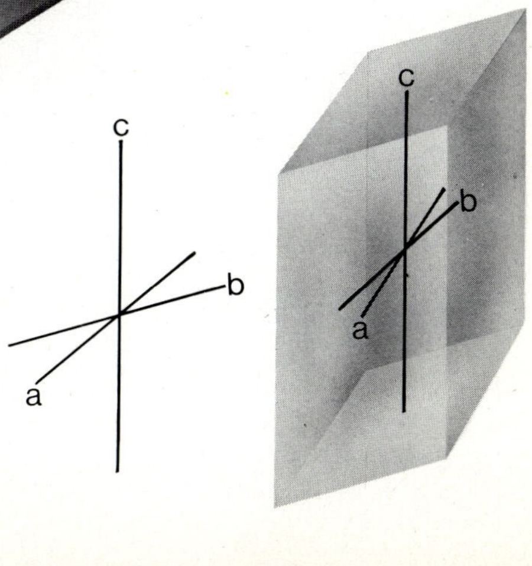

1

2. JASPER *Devon.* Jasper is the name given to a large family of rocks of wide-ranging appearance and texture. When earlier earthy or clayey material becomes cemented by silica and coloured by impurities, the product is a jasper. Since the original material will be largely silicate, jasper is an impure, coloured, opaque quartz. High-grade lapidary jaspers, as in the illustration, derive from very fine-grain source rocks, often china clay.

2

1. HAEMATITE (Kidney ore) *Cumberland.* **SPECULARITE.**
Haematite is a common mineral, though infrequently found in its well-crystallised forms. It has wide-ranging appearances and physical properties. Cumberland provides black gem quality cutting material. Kidney ore is the interesting example in the (reniform) crystal habit. Specularite is the spectacular brilliant, thin black plates form of haematite.

Properties: OXIDE – Ferric iron oxide.

Crystal system: Hexagonal but wide range of crystal habits including thick tabular crystals, thin plates and reniform. Colour red to black; streak bright red; hardness 1–6·5; density 4·9–5·3; fracture conchoidal, no cleavage.

Formative environment: Haematite is usually of sedimentary origin though commonly metamorphic. A common soil colorant due to the breakdown of other iron-bearing minerals.

3. BUTTERFLIES IN ORNAMENTAL STONE. Examples of lapidary work employing various rocks as ornamental stones. The top butterfly is fashioned from actinolite, and the bottom moth is serpentine. A rough quartz pebble (with natural lichens growing on it) provides the base.

4. CHALCEDONY *Cornwall.*
Chalcedony is one of the 'cryptocrystalline' forms of quartz. These forms appear as massive but are crystalline at the sub-microscopic level. Other chalcedonic forms of quartz include flint, chert, carnelian, chrysoprase and agate.

Properties: OXIDE – Silicon dioxide.

Crystal system: Cryptocrystalline, waxy appearance, transparent to translucent. Forms stalactitic (as illustration) or botryoidal masses. Hardness 7; density 2·6–2·64; fracture conchoidal.

Formative environment: Occurs as linings to cavities in rocks, probably from silica gels.

5

6

5. OPAL ON QUARTZ *Cornwall.* Opal is related to quartz, being silicon dioxide plus up to 10 per cent water. Precious opal (opal exhibiting the prized 'fire' optical effect) has probably not been found in Britain. Common opal (illustrated) is prized for its usual intense yellow/green fluorescence.

Properties: OXIDE – Hydrated silicon dioxide.

Crystal system: Amorphous, no crystal structure, forms in cavities and seams. Sometimes pseudomorphous after wood, bones and shells, etc. Colourless to lightly coloured, the gem variety exhibiting the rainbow colour play (opalescence); hardness 5–6; density 1·9–2·2; fracture conchoidal.

Formative environment: Always deposited at low temperatures from silica-bearing solutions. Frequently found in hot springs, recently volcanoes and sediments.

7

6. NATIVE COPPER *Ireland.* Copper is commonly used in jewellery work for its warm colour. Some jewellers create designs round uncut gem crystals or native metallic clusters of gold, silver or copper.

Properties: NATIVE ELEMENT – Copper plus traces.

Crystal system: Cubic but often in 'hackly' masses. Copper coloured, metallic; hardness 2·5–3; density 8·7; malleable and ductile.

Formative environment: Always metamorphic in altered sulphide veins, volcanic rocks or, rarely, secondary sedimentary deposits.

7. QUARTZ CRYSTAL *Cornwall.* Quartz is the most abundant mineral species. It forms a family of minerals, initially, divided between crystalline and cryptocrystalline varieties. Some of the crystalline varieties are named on a basis of colour – water clear (rock crystal), white (milky quartz), yellow (citrine), brown (smoky quartz), violet (amethyst), black (morion).

Properties: OXIDE – Silicon dioxide.

Crystal system: Hexagonal, usual habit hexagonal prism with terminating pyramid. Sometimes doubly terminated (see illustration). Transparent to translucent. Colourless to coloured; glassy; hardness 7; density 2·6; fracture conchoidal.

8. WOOD TIN *Cornwall.* Wood tin is a rare form of cassiterite (tin ore) where the cassiterite has formed radiating, botryoidal structures in a quartz vein rock. Cut and polished slices of wood tin (see illustration) are attractive ornamental stone. During Cornwall's eighteenth- and nineteenth-century mining heyday, wood tin was prized for cutting and jewellery work, especially in mining families. Today, high cost associated with rarity and geological interest prevent any large-scale employment of wood tin.
Properties: OXIDE – Tin dioxide

9. AMETHYST CRYSTAL GROUP. Amethyst is the 'glamour-girl' of the quartz family. The well-known lilac to deep violet coloured crystals have always attracted jewellers' attention. The specimen illustrated is a fine old-time example of a geode (crystal-lined cavity) from the long-closed Levant Tin Mine at St Just in Cornwall. Amethyst derives its colour from the presence of minute impurities of manganese and iron that modify quartz's optical properties.
Properties: OXIDE – Silicon dioxide.

10. MALACHITE Botryoidal and Polished. Malachite has recently experienced a large-scale return to popularity in jewellery and artistic work. None of the present-day British sources provide suitable quality malachite in commercial quantities. The examples illustrated are nineteenth-century Cornish.
Properties: CARBONATE – Basic copper carbonate.
Crystal system: Monoclinic but rarely crystalline. Most malachite crystals are azurite pseudomorphs. Usually forms as silky crusts or botryoidal masses (see illustration). Light to dark green; streak pale; vitreous; hardness 3·5-4; density 3·9-4; basal cleavage, splintery fracture.
Formative environment: Always metamorphic in altered sulphide veins or secondary sedimentary sediments.

9

10

11. SMOKY QUARTZ GROUP *Cornwall.* Smoky quartz varies between sherry colour to dark brown. Although found in almost every environment, the really fine examples are usually limited to veins in igneous rocks or pegmatic veins. The fine example illustrated is a recent find from a quartz vein in a Cornish china clay pit. The smoky colour is due to traces of iron, but very dark tones may also be due to close proximity of radio-active minerals.
Properties: OXIDE– Silicon dioxide.

12a. TOURMALINE *Devon.* There are several varieities of tourmaline with varying colours and composition. Schorl (illustrated) black, rubelite red, indicolite blue. Jewellers label the green, tourmaline.
Properties: SILICATE – Complex Boro-silicate.
Crystal system: Hexagonal, usually near-triangular prisms. Colours various; lustre glassy; hardness 7–7.5; density 3–3.3; fracture conchoidal; cleavage poor.

12b. SPHALERITE on DOLOMITE *Ireland.* Sphalerite is a common mineral and the main ore of zinc. 'Gemmy' sphalerite, as illustrated, is rare, only Santander in Spain being a noted locality. When cut, gem sphalerite is pleasing, but its tendency to cleave and limited hardness prevent its popular acceptance by jewellers.
Properties: SULPHIDE – Zinc sulphide.
Crystal system: Cubic, well-formed crystals common. Colourless through tints of yellow, red, brown to black; streak pale; lustre resinous; hardness 3.5–4; fracture conchoidal; perfect cleavage.
Formative environment: Sulphide ore veins occurring in all rock types.

13a. PREHNITE *Isle of Skye.* Prehnite is not uncommon as infilling in the cavities of basic rocks. Like serpentine, it is seldom seen in mass-produced work. Good quality, transparent green prehnite produces excellent gemstones and the translucent yellow/green material carves well.
Properties: SILICATE – Hydrous calcium aluminium silicate.
Crystal system: Orthorhombic but crystals rare and small. Occurs as transparent to translucent yellow/green botryoidal masses; lustre glassy; hardness 6–6.5; density 2.8–2.9; fracture uneven; basal cleavage.
Formative environment: Fills cavities in old lavas and basic rocks due to hot solutions attacking and altering earlier minerals.

13b. GARNET *Devon.* Garnets comprise a family of six related sub-species and numerous varietal forms. All species have been found in gem quality. Glossularite (illustrated) has a range of pale colours (excluding reds). The light orange/brown examples are called 'cinnamon stone', but it is the pale greens that name the species; glossular is the botanical name for the gooseberry. Massive glossularite is carved in Burma as jade; carved South African massive glossularite is sold as South African jade.

Properties: SILICATE – Calcium aluminium silicate.

Crystal system: Cubic, well-formed crystals common especially dodecahedron form. Colours pale green, cinnamon and other pale tints excluding reds; lustre glassy; hardness 6–7·5; density 3·5–4·3; fracture conchoidal; no cleavage.

Formative environment: Garnets as a group are common minerals but are either pegmatic or metamorphic in origin. Glossularite, being a calcium garnet, forms in metamorphosed lime-rich rocks. Almandine (illustration 14) forms where iron minerals are present and notable in mica schist.

12a   12b

13a   13b

14. GARNETS in Hornfelse *Cornwall*. **GARNET** on Schist. Almandine garnets (illustrated) are the familiar red/violet semi-precious gems of commercial jewellery. The small almandines imbedded into hornfelse (highly metamorphosed sediment) are a Cornish example from Botallack Cliff. The large single crystal on mica schist is Scottish.

Properties: SILICATE – Iron aluminium silicate.

Crystal system: Cubic, well-formed crystals common especially dodecahedron form. Colour red/violet; lustre glassy; hardness 6–7.5; density 3.5–4.3; fracture conchoidal; no cleavage.

Formative environment: Pegmatic on metamorphic origin. Commonly found in metamorphosed sediments, i.e., mica schists.

15. PEGMATITE with **APATITE CRYSTALS** *Cornwall*. Apatite, small blue crystals, occur in numerous colours and forms. Named from the Greek – to deceive – due to similarity with other species. Coloured, transparent crystals make excellent gems though too soft for extensive commercial use.

Properties: PHOSPHATE – Calcium fluorophosphate.

Crystal system: Hexagonal, crystals frequent but wide variation in habit. Colourless, white, yellow, brown, blue, green, flesh red, violet; lustre glassy; hardness 5; density 3.1–3.2; fracture conchoidal; slight cleavage.

Formative environment: Distributed grains of apatite occur in many rock types and massive consolidations occur in igneous rocks. Crystalline specimens form in pegmatites. (See pegmatite, illustration 22.)

16. IRON PYRITE *Cornwall*. Well-crystallised and lustrous iron pyrite is popular for decor pieces and inclusion in jewellery. An abundant mineral, frequently well crystallised, but little has the necessary lustre and tarnish resistance.

Properties: SULPHIDE – Iron sulphide.

Crystal system: Cubic, well-formed cubes, pyritohedrons and octohedrons found. Light yellow, metallic lustre; hardness 6–6.5; density 5; fracture conchoidal; cleavage none.

Formative environment: An abundant species occurring in all types of rock and mineral veins.

15

16

17. QUARTZ, JASPER, SERPENTINE *Cornwall.* Serpentine properly is a single mineral species. The very varied rock type – serpentine – is a mixture of serpentine and various secondary minerals. As a cutting material and ornamental stone, serpentine is locally popular. Much so-called jade and marble, including verde-antique and Connemara marble, is in fact serpentine rock. Precious serpentine is crystallised peridot. The polished slices illustrated are attractive Cornish serpentines with quartz and jasper infillings.

Properties: SILICATE – Hydrous magnesium silicate.

Crystal system: No crystal form, always amorphous masses of red, black, brown, yellow, green; lustre waxy to greasy; hardness 2–5; density 2·2–2·6; no cleavage.

Formative environment: Always metamorphic resulting from the action of hot solutions altering earlier igneous rocks, usually peridotites.

18. FLUORSPAR and **GALENA** *Cumberland.* Fluorspar is a collector's mineral. Occurring in a wide range of colours and, frequently, spectacular crystal groups. The Cumberland green and blue/green examples are world classics. Occasionally cut as a gem it is too soft for general use. The Chinese carve the green material as green quartz. The splendid mauve group illustrated is a decor piece. Blue John (see illustration 32) is the distinctive Derbyshire variety.

Properties: HALIDE – Calcium Fluoride.

Crystal system: Cubic, perfect cubes common. Almost every colour and shade reported; lustre glassy; hardness 4; density 3–3·3; fracture conchoidal; perfect cleavage.

Formative environment: Found in sedimentary and igneous rocks as ore veins, mineralised joints and pegmatite veins. Both high and low temperature environments.

19a. LAVENDER AMETHYST with **GOETHITE** inclusions *Cornwall.* Pale lilac amethyst crystals on serpentine. Each crystal contains a minute inclusion in the form of a 'golden dart' of the mineral goethite.

Properties: OXIDE – Silicon dioxide.

19b. TOURMALINATED QUARTZ *Cornwall.* Tourmalinated quartz, clear massive quartz with needle-like crystal inclusions of black tourmaline (schorl). Quartz not infrequently provides examples of natural encapsulation by crystallising around earlier formed crystals. Other typical examples are goethite (illustration 19a), rutile and the green mineral chlorite (moss agate).

19a   19b

20a 20b

21

20a. BERYL CRYSTALS *Ireland.* Large gem quality beryls are not reported from the British Isles. Small transparent crystals and larger opaque ones, though, occur in Ireland, Scotland and Cornwall. The gem varieties of beryl are emerald (green), aquamarine (blue) golden beryl (yellow-brown), morganite (pink).

Properties: SILICATE – Beryllium aluminium silicate.

Crystal system: Hexagonal prisms usual. White, yellow, blue, green and pink; lustre glassy; hardness 8; density 2·6–2·8; fracture conchoidal; cleavage poor.

Formative environment: Usually pegmatite veins.

20b. CELESTITE *Gloucestershire.* Celestite's fine light blue crystals are occasionally faceted though rather soft and liable to cleave. Crystal-lined cavities are attractive collector's and decor pieces.

Properties: SULPHATE – Strontium sulphate.

Crystal system: Orthorhombic, tabular crystals common. Colourless, white, brown or blue; lustre glassy; hardness 3–3·5; density 3·9–4; fracture uneven; strong cleavage.

21. SERPENTINES *Cornwall.* Selection of cut slices of unusual serpentine. The white ingredient is steatite.

Properties: SILICATE – Hydrous magnesium silicate.

22. PEGMATITE *Cornwall.* Pegmatites are unusual magmatic rocks characterised by large, often well-crystallised minerals. They form as dykes and veins in magmatic rocks or the surrounding rocks. Their special character derives, in part, from the presence of rare elements like lithum, beryllium, fluorine and boron. The presence of these 'exotic' elements results in the formation of unusual minerals, notably several species of precious stones. Excluding diamond and the oxide gems – ruby and sapphire – most of the world's precious stones form in pegmatites. In the illustration are feldspar, smoky quartz, tourmaline and mica crystals. Compare also illustrations 15 and 34.

23a   **23b**

23a. NATIVE COPPER *Cornwall.* Highly decorative polished slice of serpentine rock displaying a band of metallic native copper. Also present: cuprite (copper oxide – purple) and chrysocolla (copper silicate – green).

23b. CHRYSOCOLLA *Cornwall.* Jewellery chrysocolla, free of flaws, is attractive cutting material. The frequent presence of quartz improves the material's hardness and lustre. Pale blue material closely resembles turquoise (see illustration 24).
Properties: SILICATE – Hydrous copper silicate.
Crystal system: Cryptocrystalline, usually forms solid or earthy vein fillings. Occasionally botryoidal or enamel-like. Colour variable, on single examples pale blue to green; lustre vitreous to earthy; hardness 2–4; density 2–2·4; fracture conchoidal.
Formative environment: Alteration band of copper deposits.

24. TURQUOISE *Cornwall.* The finest jewellery turquoise comes from Iran and Tibet, though quantities of lower-grade material are mined in Chile and the United States. The sole British locality to date reported is Cornwall. Turquoise has been a noted mineral in the Gunheath China Clay Pit for several decades. In 1976 the author identified another Cornish source.
Properties: PHOSPHATE – Hydrous basic aluminium phosphate – plus copper.
Crystal system: Triclinic but crystals very rare and small. Usual form thin seams and crusts. Colour sky blue to greenish blue; streak pale; lustre porcelaneous; hardness 5–6; density 2·6–2·8; fracture smooth.
Formative environment: Always metamorphic forming in alumina-rich rocks usually in arid climates.

25. TOPAZ Pebble and cut Topaz *Cornwall.* Precious minerals, due to their characteristic hardness, have great ability to survive erosional processes. Precious minerals, notably diamond, ruby, sapphire, emerald and topaz, are frequently transported distances from their formative source and incorporated into alluvial deposits, i.e. gem gravels. The large, worn topaz crystal illustrated was found in a 'raised beach' of Pliocene date on the Cornish coast. Since the crystal was of Scottish, or Scandinavian, origin it was presumably carried on an ancient ice floe. The small pale blue faceted topaz is included for comparison.

24

25

27. SEMI-PRECIOUS GEMSTONES. A selection of semi-precious cut stones. Faceted, cabachon cut and shaped pendant pieces. Rock crystal (water clear), citrine (yellow to golden brown), smoky quartz (dark brown), amethyst (lilac to violet), carnelian (orange translucent), agate (banded colours), garnet (deep red). Note that all are in the quartz family except the garnet.

28a   **28b**

26. AZURITE Wales. **AZURITE** Ireland. Azurite, like its close relative malachite, is increasingly exciting the interest of jewellers, especially craftsmen who create individual pieces. Unlike malachite, which is rarely crystalline, azurite is often found in well-crystallised forms. It is never faceted or cabochoned; whole, small crystal beds are trimmed and incorporated into jewllery.

Properties: CARBONATE – Basic copper carbonate.

Crystal system: Monoclinic, brilliant blue crystals common, often partially altered into malachite. Colour azure blue; streak pale; lustre glassy; hardness 3·5–4; density 3·8; fracture conchoidal; pronounced cleavage.

Formative environment: As for malachite (illustration 10) altered sulphide veins or secondary deposits.

28a. CUPRITE Cornwall. Cuprites' wine-red crystals inspired the old miners' name for it – Ruby Copper. Occasionally, large transparent crystals have been faceted; more often massive translucent material is cabochoned. Cuprite is never a commercial gemstone. Frequently associated with native copper (see illustration 23a).

Properties: OXIDE – Cuprous oxide.

Crystal system: Cubic and well-developed cubic or octahedral crystals are common. Also forms as crystalline masses. Colour cochineal red to dark red; lustre adamantine; hardness 3·5–4; density 5·8–6·1; fracture conchoidal; poor cleavage.

Formative environment: Alteration zone of sulphide copper ore bodies.

28b. CHALCOPYRITE Cornwall. Chalcopyrite has a characteristic rainbow iridescent tarnish, hence the name Peacock Ore. Although always opaque it makes attractive jewellery.

Properties: SULPHIDE – Iron copper sulphide.

Crystal system: Tetragonal, crystals not uncommon. Colour (fresh break) golden; lustre metallic often exhibiting iridescent tarnish; hardness 3·5–4; density 4·1–4·3; fracture uneven; cleavage poor.

Formative environment: Found commonly in sulphide veins and as grains in many types of rocks.

29. AMETHYST. Cabochon cut amethyst crystal mounted into an original craftsman-made silver pendant.

30. LUXULYANITE *Cornwall.* The attractive cut and polished slice of ornamental stone is Luxulyanite. Almost the total quantity of this rare rock was used in the creation of the Duke of Wellington's sarcophagus in Westminster Abbey. Luxulyanite takes its name from the nearby village and is a metamorphosed granite. The pink phenocrysts are orthoclase feldspar and the green intergrowths tourmaline.

31. MALACHITE cabochons. A selection of variously shaped malachite cabochons ready for incorporation into jewellery pieces. The malachite employed in these items was recently mined in South-West Africa. No current British locality is producing commercial quantities of suitable quality material.

30

31

32

32. FLUORSPAR variety Blue John *Derbyshire*. Blue John, the familiar deep purple banded variety of fluorspar from Derbyshire has long been in demand for artistic work. Formerly, when the best quality unflawed and deeply coloured material was abundant, there was a sizeable associated local cutting industry. Small quantities are still mined/collected and cut for trinkets and jewellery cabochons.
Properties: HALIDE – Calcium fluoride.

33a 33b

33a. CALCITE variety Travertine *Somerset*. Travertine is a massive recrystallised variety of calcite. Its banded and layered structure results from the variation in impurity content in successive layers of the deposited material. It is soft and easily polished, even by hand, and much used for the production of tourist souvenirs. Natural and dyed material is frequently misrepresented as onyx, jade, alabaster, marble, etc.

Properties: CARBONATE – Calcium carbonate.

Crystal system: Hexagonal, crystals common with a wide range of forms. Colourless to all pale tints; lustre glassy; hardness 3; density 2·7; fracture conchoidal; marked cleavage.

Formative environment: Calcite occurs in every type of environment and in every rock type.

33b. RHODONITE *Cornwall*. Rhodonite of suitable quality and appearance is used both as an ornamental stone for cutting and carving and as a jewellery semi-precious stone. Being opaque it is always cabochon cut.

Properties: SILICATE – Manganese silicate.

Crystal system: Triclinic but crystals rare and small. Colour pink usually with black patches; lustre glassy; hardness 5·5–6; density 3·4–3·7; fracture splintery; cleavage when heated to about 90 °C.

Formative environment: A manganese ore occurring in metamorphic rocks especially in manganese-bearing ore veins.

34. TOPAZ crystals on **PEGMATITE** *Ireland*. Topaz is a valuable precious mineral much used in jewellery. The pale blue and the golden-brown (noble) topaz are most highly valued. Fine, though usually small, topaz crystals occur in Scotland, Ireland and Cornwall. Massive topaz is also found in metamorphosed granitic rocks.

Properties: SILICATE – Aluminium fluorosilicate.

Crystal system: Orthorhombic, commonly in well-formed crystals. Colourless, white, pale blue, yellow, green, brown and pink; lustre glassy; hardness 8; density 3·5–3·6; fracture conchoidal; perfect basal cleavage.

Formative environment: Pegmatic dykes and veins, and veins in granitic rocks and alteration veins.

35

35. DIOPTASE (Emerald copper) *Unlocated.* Dioptase's beautiful, emerald-green crystals immediately suggest a jewellery application, but the mineral is rare. There are no present-day British sources except a lucky find on an old mine dump. Formerly dioptase (emerald copper) was noted in some Cornish copper mines. The principal present-day source is South-West Africa.

Properties: SILICATE – Hydrous copper silicate.

Crystal system: Hexagonal, usually well crystallised in short prisms. Colour emerald green; lustre glassy; hardness 5; density 3·3–3·4; fracture uneven to conchoidal; perfect cleavage.

Formative environment: Alteration zone of copper ores.

36. DIAMOND TIN (Cassiterite) *Cornwall.* Cassiterite is tin ore. Usually massive or impregnating other rocks. The spectacular brilliant, transparent, dark-coloured crystals from the St Agnes area in Cornwall were dubbed diamond tin and sometimes fashioned into jewellery locally.

Properties: OXIDE – Tin dioxide.

Crystal system: Tetragonal and often in well-formed crystals. Colour yellow through red/brown tones to black; streak white; lustre adamantine; hardness 6–7; density 6·8–7·1; fracture conchoidal; poor cleavage. (See also illustration 8.)

Formative environment: Pegmatite dykes and veins, and high temperature veins.

36